Gifts Without Wrapping

First published 2019 by The Hedgehog Poetry Press

Published in the UK by
The Hedgehog Poetry Press
Coppack House, 5
Churchill Avenue
Clevedon
BS21 6QW

www.hedgehogpress.co.uk

ISBN: 978-1-9160908-6-6

Copyright © Michał Choiński 2019

Cover art by Jakub Sokólski.

The right of Michał Choiński to be identified as the author of this work has been asserted in accordance with the Copyright, Designs and Patents Act 1988.

All rights reserved. No part of this publication may be reproduced, stored in or introduced into a retrieval system, or transmitted in any form, or by any means (electronic, mechanical, photocopying, recording or otherwise) without prior written permissions of the publisher. Any person who does any unauthorised act in relation to this publication may be liable for criminal prosecution and civil claims for damages,

9 8 7 6 5 4 3 2 1

A CIP Catalogue record for this book is available from the British Library.

Contents

The Prototype	7
The Full Moon	8
The Climb	9
Commemoration	10
The Unwrapping	11
Fear of Lepidopterism	12
Doing Business	13
The Terminus	14
My True Love	15
The Liturgy of the Flesh	16

Gifts Without Wrapping

by

Michał Choiński

THE PROTOTYPE

The proportions were everything,
I was told by the guide,
as she walked past the prototype,
pointing out the features, here and there
I would probably miss on my own.
The body is measured by itself,
six palms make up one unit,
she continued, a closed circuit of beauty.
The fact that the statue lacked one arm,
and the nose, and the genitals, and a toe,
was immaterial to her.
I presume, it is the idea of him she was after.

I visualize her in the evening, after work,
home alone,
as she fantasizes about the statue complete.
She imagines different body supplements,
as if she were trying on different sets of gloves,
that can never fit in just right.
I imagine her wishing she herself
were of marble,
but incomplete, a work in progress,
whose promise of perfection,
does not deter others from touching
the form of the idea.

THE FULL MOON

The power of this first encounter
takes me by surprise,
but to you it is just a manifestation
of how our bodies cannot resist
being driven by the moon.

The pouring of wine takes time,
so we talk
of those we have abandoned.
And when you sip from the glass,
I watch your lips, all in red.
But your eyes are somewhere else.
So, from where I sit, I can relish
but a fraction of your full image.

The taste of that lukewarm claret
still lingers on, while the dead listen in
on how we discuss the coming tide,
and how words passed from mouth to mouth,
like a candy during a kiss,
bring us far more pleasure than they should.

THE CLIMB

She claimed she could sniff everything out,
and I thought it was just a tease.
But, on the track to Banówka,
as we walked,
gazing at the mountain view,
she said she could smell
more than I could see,
that all the chopped trees smell to her
the same way dead bodies smell to me,
and that in the city public toilets are disorienting –
"A territory marked by everybody", she said.
I contributed little,
panting heavily when we ascended,
as the path seemed
increasingly challenging.
She said one sniff was enough to see
if she liked any male body,
and I began to wonder
if this was her pick-up line.
But it wasn't,
because
when I slowed down,
she speeded up,
pacing, skipping
and skittering.
Out of breath, I took a break.
And then she left me there,
though she promised she'd collect me
on her way back from the top.

COMMEMORATION

Over Kasia's bed hung the image
of Saint Catherine's head,
dried up, covered in red rose petals.
She got it from her aunt in Tuchów,
and brought it over, to remember.
"I want to lose control", she declared,
thwarting his plans of withdrawal.
And he knew that when
a body becomes a body,
the dignity of the ritual
requires the myrrh to be burnt,
and then nobody
can resist fear and trembling.
And when the borders of bodies
reveal themselves
as neither stiff, nor sealed,
they soon collapse
into different signifiers,
like inexperienced lovers,
lost in a jungle of limbs.
And then, looking up,
he remembered
that even the unspeakably repulsive
have their saint,
who also oversees coffeehouses.
The busiest one of all.

THE UNWRAPPING

The sweetest taste is the smell of the skin
freshly bathed in the milk of the lamb;
the fragrance poised to attract the prey,
to lure it into a hideout where
shades are opulent, but never menacing.
The wildest night is with a girl whose left thigh
is marked by a tattoo in the shape of a tiger,
fearful and symmetrical, jumping out at you,
in the midst of the act, marking your back
with its claw's quick scratch.
And once you get that stigma, and wrap
yourself in your clothes again, relishing
the metallic, salty taste in your mouth,
you are out into the open,
to eat or to be eaten.

FEAR OF LEPIDOPTERISM

When asked about how things were,
she'd give you answers like,
"I'm OK, but did you know
that butterflies drink turtle tears
to replace sodium?"
But in bed, she transformed
into a different form.
There, I'd relish every bead of sweat
coming from her temple,
down her cheeks,
reaching her dimple.
When she crossed the wrists
of her clenched fists
on a pillow,
they really looked like a butterfly.
And when she cried with joy,
watching nature documentaries,
I was often tempted to taste her tears.
Yet, I was afraid my body would not take them in –
I imagined my skin red with irritation,
and my eyes glassy, almost breakable.
So, I withdrew,
letting her fantasize in solitude
about her pending metamorphosis.

DOING BUSINESS

Our love was never contractual,
and yet, we bartered
gifts, like two totalitarian leaders
at a political summit,
before they do business.
The perimeters of her body,
were strategically delineated.
A detailed map was sketched,
demarcating all the landmarks.
Like, she had this funny mark
on her belly that looked like a cherry.
She commanded me to hate it,
but I simply could not perform
this act of malice on her idiosyncrasy.
Yet, my resistance was feeble.
She broke me at the twilight.
I declared my loathing
in spite of all my love,
as if she held a gun to my head.

THE TERMINUS

"*Soy Gitano*" she said, taking her dress off.
"*Ja też*", I replied.
Then she lit scented candles
to cover up the smell of sweat.
It is her body she mistrusted,
not mine,
and it is the scoliosis on her back
I saw more often,
than her gorgeous gnathion.
Her body felt
like a dead body,
a sympathetic gift
from a willing soul.
Because she invited me
to nest with her,
before moving on,
she remained
satisfied with how we mixed tongues,
and with that desperate equilibrium
of flesh,
we were given to celebrate
for a while,
before
the termination.

MY TRUE LOVE

I run because I love
examining how my sinews
increase the momentum,
propelling me to sprint,
and because I adore
observing how I sweat
from the pores
located all over my skin.
My most important muscle,
is not my heart,
but the gluteus maximus,
which makes me bipedal,
and gives me the power
to sprint.

When I run, I love
monitoring how my eyebrows
prevent the sweat
from invading my eyes.
With the 37th kilometre,
I turn –
my nipples bleed
unaccustomed to the friction
of clothing,
and, shedding all decorum,
I begin inspecting
all involuntary secretions.

If I could, I'd love
to prostrate myself
on an autopsy table,
and cut deeper,
to comprehend
all somatic nuances
of how I run,
and maybe to put together
a poem about love
for running..

THE LITURGY OF THE FLESH

In November, in Poland,
when the drivers honk like madmen,
you often fantasize
about the end of the world.
Daydreaming about love and hate,
not about forgiveness,
but about the punishment.
You imagine how fire shall consume it all,
and how all shall perish and wither away.
The sinful to pay for their disobedience,
the faithful to be rewarded for restraint.
All to be resurrected upon the end,
led by that sound of the trumpeter.

All the masses for the people long lost,
paid for with money wrapped in envelopes,
with faith that what is invested here
will bring profits there,
and that the body is not lost, but will be made anew
for those who knew how to use it well.
Luca Signorelli painted the scene,
showing how they hoist each other up,
proud of being flesh again,
and Jorie Graham gave it voice,
describing the master,
who dissects and penetrates.
But my mind cannot simply mend itself,
buried in the open flesh, like a snail.